Are You Making Money? Modern Artists Handbook – Vol 5

Are You Making Money?

Modern Artists Handbook #5

Gail Daley

Are You Making Money? Modern Artists Handbook – Vol 5

E-book ISBN: 9781386437130
Print ISBN- 9781393931393
ASIN:

For permission requests, write to the publisher, addressed "Attention: Permissions Coordinator," at the address below.

Gail Daley
5688 E Sussex Way
Fresno, CA 93727
www.gaildaleysfineart.com

Bulk Sales Ordering Information: Quantity sales. Special discounts are available on quantity purchases by corporations, associations, and others. For details, contact the "Bulk Sales Department" at the address above.

Publisher's Note: This is a work of fiction, and any resemblance to any persons living or dead is unintentional and accidental.

Names, characters, places, and incidents are a product of the author's imagination. Locales and public names are sometimes used for atmospheric purposes. Any resemblance to actual people, living or dead, or to businesses, companies, events, institutions, or locales is completely coincidental.

DISCLAIMER

The information in this booklet is for general information purposes only; it is not intended to be tax or legal advice. Each situation is specific; consult your CPA or attorney to discuss your specific requirements or questions

Are You Making Money? Modern Artists Handbook – Vol 5

Are You Making Money? Modern Artists Handbook – Vol 5

Table of Contents

INTRODUCTION

Most of us create because we need it. It is also nice if our creations can become our life’s work and support us. This volume was designed to help an artist, photographer, writer or fine art crafter figure out how to make their passion pay for itself.

Please note, anything covered here is NOT to be taken as legally binding. In other words, If I mention a website, or suggest a method or means to accomplish your goal, it is only a suggestion. I made these suggestions from my personal experience and what did or did not work for me. If something doesn’t work for you, go find something that does.

CHOOSING AN EVENT TO ATTEND

As an artist just beginning to sell your work, the more visible your art is, the potential collectors will see it and talk about it, and perhaps buy it! You need to get your name out there. The more potential buyers who have seen your work, the more they will talk about it! Art & Craft Fairs and Festivals can be an important sales tool for artists and writers. One of the simplest ways to meet potential customers is go participate in local events where buyers can see and purchase your work. These festivals and fairs come in all sizes and locations, and the quality of the fair itself as well as the artists who attend can be widely different, so choose your event wisely. To make a good choice, you will need to decide on many things; how many of these events you can afford to attend, how far you want to travel, how much physical work will be needed at the event and are you capable of performing it.

QUESTIONS TO ASK

Before choosing to participate in an event, it is important to ask at least some of the questions below rom the event promoters:

How much are the entry fees? If the fee is too high you may not make a profit, even if you make sales.

What was the average sales volume by exhibitors in past years?

How many years has this event been in existence? A brand-new event will have to do more advertising in order to bring in crowds.

Who attends the event? I.e., what economic demographic is the event aimed at? This is very important, because an event aimed at a lower income demographic, may not draw attendees who will buy original art.

What Press Releases are going to be sent out, and to whom?

Is it easy to find? Are there signs or billboards along the road leading to the event?

Will the event be indoors or outdoors?

How physically difficult will it be to bring in your work and set up? If you can drive your vehicle directly into the booth area, it makes it much easier to unload and set up your work.

How much time will you have to set up your booth?

Is there parking for vendors and attendees?

How attractive is the area where the event will take place? An unattractive area or an area with a bad local reputation may not draw the type of crowd you will be looking for.

What type of security is there for vendors and for the event itself?

What is the geographic location of the event?

Ideally, an event site should be well kept up with good parking for both attendees and vendors (that's you!). Art Buyers are attracted to spacious and elegant spaces (convention centers, high-end hotels, museums or community centers).

What artists are attending these events and how well known are they? Is this the first year this artist has attended this event? If well-known artists are long-time attenders of the event, it is a good bet that they are making enough sales to justify returning each year.

What type of art sells well at this event? Is it the same type as yours? For instance, an event geared toward a certain subject matter or art style is going to attract collectors of that type of art. If you create exclusively illustrations, an event geared towards impressionist painting probably isn't the right venue for you.

Finally, before jumping in, visit the event at least once before signing up as a vendor. Talk to the other artists and find out what their opinion of the event is. Do they think it is well run? Are they making money? Would they come back next year?

EXCELLENT OKAY POOR

10	9	8	7	6	5	4	3	2	1	
										Was the event well run?
										Was there enough advertising?
										Were they in a good location to attract buyers?
										Was the event easy for the public to find?
										Were the other vendors happy?
										How large were the crowds?
										Did they make sales?

During your visit, ask the other vendors these questions and keep a running total of the answers.

THE IDEAL EVENT

I call Art, Craft Fairs & Festivals or Book Signings “Booth Events” because usually you set up your own sales booth. Generally, there are 3 types of these events Outdoor, Indoor and Tabletop and Events can be geared to sell only art or allow different types of vendors, and they can be “juried or non-juried”. If an event is “juried”, then you usually must submit photos of your work and/or your display set up to a panel, who then decide if your work will do credit to their event. Typically, these events cost more in entry fees, but they also draw a more “art-oriented” crowd who are more likely to buy your work. When checking out a juried event, make sure the information you submit concerning your work and your display meets their requirements! The quality of the art and consequently the potential buyers is likely to be higher at juried art and craft shows.

The very best types of events are those that sell only art. Some of the events where only art is sold like the one in Laguna Nigel, CA are juried. They are expensive and hard to get into, but when you do, they attract art buyers or at least folks who came to look at art. In the San Joaquin Valley where I live, events that sell only art are rare, but some venues that attract multiple types of items are complimentary to art sales. If possible, you should try to match your art to the target audience. Wine tasting events put on by the local wineries are usually inexpensive to join. Still lifes using wine, grapes or vineyards, and people drinking wine usually sell well. If you are a pet artist, find out when the local kennel club or SPCA is having an event and set up there. If you do a lot of western art, check out the local rodeo.

Non-juried events may be geared toward a more general economic demographic and not draw in the art collectors and buyers you are looking for. A huge event like Big Hat Days in Clovis, CA will also be expensive.

Sure, Big Hat Days will attract 10,000 people, but most of them didn't come to look at art, and if they do buy art, chances are it will be from the cut-rate art broker in the next aisle who is ***not*** selling his own work.

Most important, before deciding to go back next year make sure you made money or at least broke even.

Total Expenses	**($844.60)**
Profit	
· · Gross Sales	**$1,500.00**
· · Sales Tax collected	**$123.38**
· · Commission (sometimes an event requires a commission on your sales or a donation of some type)	**($150.00)**
Gross Profit	**$1,473.38**
Net Profit	**$628.78**

OUTDOOR EVENTS

Outdoor events are usually larger than the Indoor ones and attract a larger crowd. A Tabletop can be either indoors or outdoors; the main difference between a Tabletop and the others is the space size. Most booth events allow you a 10’ x 10’ space. With a tabletop you have a space about the length and width of a table (usually 8' long by 3' wide) to display your work.

Outdoor venues are likely to cost more to enter than tabletops. Indoor event entry costs vary widely, depending on what group is organizing it. Even if you live in a mild climate like California, these different events are seasonal. Outdoor events usually take place in the Spring, Summer or Early Fall. FYI unless the event is an art-only event the crowd is unlikely to made up of serious art collectors and you will probably be competing with the vendor who brought in mass produced canvas paintings. In this type of event, I would recommend setting up to create a painting or offering to do quick sketches to attract people to your booth. You should also have a number of small ticket items for sale at events like these: cards, small prints, bookmarks, etc.

WHAT TO BRING

Pop-Up booth: Pop-Ups come in several price ranges and styles. Ideally, you will have help setting it up, but I would recommend the E-Z Up brand with the white top because it can be set up by one person. If you have never set up a booth, I recommend a couple of practice trials setting it up in your yard before you go out to the event. The best Pop-Ups for displaying art have white top and straight sides. The white top provides more light to see the art and the straight sides give you somewhere to fasten display racks. You can also purchase sidewalls to hang from the sides of the booth, which are necessary if you are taking part in an event that lasts several days; you can use the sidewalls to enclose the booth when you go home for the night. FYI, unless the event has very good security, I wouldn't recommend leaving your work out, but you can leave your display stands set up inside.

Display Stands or Racks: You can buy display set-ups from the art supply catalogs; but these can be pricey. However, it is possible to make your own. I bought 8' wire closet shelving from the local hardware store. Turned on end, they can be fastened together with plastic tie straps or Velcro, and the wire bars then make spaces to hang different sizes of art. This portable shelving can also be made into stand-alone shapes (boxes, triangles and rectangles). For indoor events where you can't take the Pop-Up, I suggest that sandbags or weighted milk cartons be fastened inside the shape to prevent tipping as additional security for stand-alone shapes.

Portable easels can also be used as a part of your display. The art supply catalogs have some excellent display easels that hold multiple pieces of art and they look very professional. You can also make display easels yourself out of copper, PVC pipe or wood; just make sure they look professional. Remember you are going to be carrying them so they should be very light weight!

Small Fold Up Tables and A Nice Tablecloth will hold your cash box and give you a hard surface when making out receipts. They can also be used to display very small or 3-deminsional art, cards, etc. Just don't make your space so crowded buyers won't enter it. In addition, if your work is light, cardboard boxes covered by tablecloths or white sheets that reach the ground look very professional and provide a good backdrop to show off your work.

Sandbags or Weights to hold down the booth in case of high winds: Weights of some kind are a must. A Pop-Up booth makes a big kite when the wind blows, and it doesn't have to be hurricane strength either. You need about 20 to 30 lbs. on each corner. Many booth events are on blacktop so you can't use the handy stakes that come with the Pop-Ups to secure your booth against winds. Sandbags are available either from the Art Supply warehouse where you got your Pop-Up or from the hardware store where you can also obtain clean, dry sand. You can also fill empty gallon milk cartons and use the handle to fasten to the legs of the booth.

Cash box a locking cash box to keep change for cash sales and checks can be bought at the local office supply store.

Chair to sit in while you will be spending a lot of time on your feet, it's nice to have a place to sit down and relax so potential buyers don't think you are just waiting to pounce.

Items To Sell Plastic boxes with good, snap-lock lids work really well to transport small items. They are waterproof and if you are doing many events, they hold up much better than cardboard. If you are going to be carrying your product in a pickup bed, make sure the lids of the boxes are fastened down and won't blow open (bungee cords work well here). You will need either bubble wrap or some type of padding to wrap around or separate delicate items. For larger pieces of art such as framed paintings or photographs, I recommend that you carry them inside your vehicle (in which case they can be separated by large pieces of cardboard to prevent scratching the frames), or completely wrapped in bubble wrap. The thing you are most looking to prevent is damage caused by the items moving around when you stop, start and turn the vehicle. I also carry either a large, wide-tip marker in either brown or black to touch up frames.

A Hand Truck You may have park some distance from your booth set up. While most places allow you to drive into the event area to set up your display, it might not be feasible for you to do so. A hand truck or dolly will enable you to haul your art, display stands and Pop-Up into the area without having to transport everything a piece at a time. This is a big plus because you may have a limited time in which to set up your booth.

A Way to Take Debit or Credit Cards If you want to make sales over $20, you will need an I-Pad, I-Phone or some other brand of smart phone and the APP enabling either Square technology or PayPal. Both companies provide a small square you can order off the internet free, attach it your smart phone or tablet it's small, portable and easy to learn to use. The company takes a small percentage of each sale as a fee (2.75% per swipe) and the money is in your account the next day. The site is https://squareup.com/ or https://paypal.com check it out. Although other companies are beginning to develop this tech, these both have a proven track record.

Sales Receipts, a calculator and bags: A receipt book is a handy way for you to keep track of cash sales. Don't spend a lot on the bags; you can get small paper bags and larger plastic ones with handles at the local Dollar Store. A small printing calculator because some customers who buy large ticket items are going to want a printed receipt, even if you are also e-mailing them one.

EVENT CHECK LIST

- POP UP BOOTH
- DISPLAY STANDS
- SMALL TABLES
- TABLECLOTHS
- SANDBAGS/WEIGHTS
- CASH BOX

- CHAIR
- ITEMS TO SELL
- A HAND TRUCK
- DEBIT CARD APP
- LAPTOBP OR TABLET
- SALES RECEIPTS
- CALCULATOR
- BAGS

INDOOR EVENTS

Requirements for an Indoor event will be slightly different from the Outdoor events. You will need everything you brought to the Outdoor event but in smaller quantities. (sales receipts, a printed calculator, your debit/credit card taker, etc.). Most indoor events will allow sellers a 10 x 10 area, but due to the inside dimensions of the event, a few of the spaces allotted aren't exactly that size or the space is not square, so there might be difficulty fitting the Pop-Up frame into the space. In addition, the top cover will keep the overhead lighting from coming through, and the ceiling in the room may not be high enough to accommodate your booth. Even if the cover is white, poor lighting will make your booth dark and unattractive. However, if the canvas or vinyl cover is removable and the ceiling is tall enough, you might still be able to use only the Pop-Up frame as a support.

Stand-alone display racks are best for an indoor event. I use 8' wire closet shelving from the local hardware store. Turned on end, they can be fastened together with plastic tie straps or Velcro, and the wire bars then make spaces to hang different sizes of art. This portable shelving can also be made into stand-alone shapes (boxes, triangles and rectangles). I suggest that sandbags or weighted milk cartons be fastened inside the shape to prevent tipping as additional security for stand-alone shapes. However, you can purchase this type of display from Art Supply catalogs and warehouses.

Portable easels can also be used as a part of your display. The art supply catalogs have some excellent display easels that hold multiple pieces of art and they look very professional. You can also make display easels yourself out of copper, PVC pipe or wood; just make sure they look professional. Remember you are going to be carrying them so they should be very light weight!

Small Folding Tables with a nice tablecloth will hold your cash box and give you a hard surface when making out receipts. They can also be used to display very small or 3-deminsional art, cards, etc. Just don’t make your space so crowded buyers won’t enter it. In addition, if your work is light, cardboard boxes covered by tablecloths or white sheets that reach the ground look very professional and provide a good backdrop to show off your work.

And of Course, don't forget the work you plan to sell!

TABLETOPS

If you do a lot of Book Signings, Church or School sponsored Boutiques, a Tabletop Event is the most common type. Tabletops occur mostly during the Holidays when many Churches and Schools use them as fund-raising events. In my opinion artists selling original art usually make very few sales. Art collectors are simply the least likely to be attracted to these fundraising everts because the majority of shoppers are looking for holiday gifts. Unless the venue attracts high income buyers most artists will find that shoppers look and admire, but don't buy. I don't say this in a negative way, but the reality is that at most of these events you will be competing with homemade crafts, make-up sales or inexpensive mass-produced decorator items.

Authors on the other hand may do well at these events because the price of a book is easily within the amount budgeted for most gifts.

At a Tabletop, you will probably be given just enough space to set up one 8'x2.5' table with room for a chair behind it, so be prepared to cut your display down and bring only what you consider the least expensive and most "sellable" items. I.E., cards, small prints, ornaments, etc.

When I go to an event, especially an Indoor event or a Tabletop, I always ask for access to electricity; I seldom take many large pieces of art to these events anymore. Since space is usually at a premium making it difficult to display a lot of large paintings; instead, I take a plug-in digital picture frame (you can do the same with either a laptop or a tablet) loaded with photos of my work. I have a power point presentation showing my work set to music. The moving slide show and music attract a lot of attention and I can display more art. Remember to have fun and talk about your work.

DOES & DON'TS

When you are attending an event, your booth or table is your store. If it isn't presented attractively, buyers will simply pass on by and you won't make sales. Make the most of the limited space you have available. Put your most eye-catching and attractive items where they will be noticed. Is your display interesting? The last page of this pamphlet has some photos of different setups used by artists at outdoor events you might want to review.

Remember that for today, *you* are the salesperson. Are you dressed to attract the kind of collector who will buy your work? If you are painting in your booth to attract a crowd, don't be afraid to look like the artist you are!

Depending on your clientele, you will need to decide whether to display pricing. Look at what the other vendors are showing in their booths and be prepared to be flexible in this area.

Make it easy to enter and exit your store. Perhaps it is a holdover from the days when humans were prey as well as predators, but no one wants to enter a space where they will be trapped. When someone enters your store, don't hover, but smile and be friendly. Talk about your work.

RE-SALE NUMBERS:

Disclaimer: The information in this booklet is for general information purposes only; it is not intended to be tax or legal advice. Each situation is specific; consult your CPA or attorney to discuss your specific requirements or questions.

Information for this section was taken from the following web sites: California State Board of Equalization (BOE) and IRS.gov. For more information or answers to specific questions, please go to those web sites.

What is a re-sale number, and why do you need one? Most sales events or venues require you to have this before they will accept you as a vendor. A re-sale number is a sales permit issued by the enabling you to engage in business in the State where the event takes place. In California, there are two types: temporary and permanent. As an artist, you normally would be considered a retailer since you sell your art directly to the public. Yes Virginia, you are required to collect sales tax on your art sales, even on commissioned art. You are also required to file the return and pay the state its due.

HOW TO APPLY FOR A SELLERS PERMIT

You can visit or call a nearby BOE office to obtain an application. Or, you can arrange to have an application mailed or faxed to you by calling **800-400-7115**. Applications can also be downloaded from the Forms and Publications Section of the BOE website.

(*Note*: You will need to mail or bring in the completed application since the BOE must have your original signature. You should make a copy for your records.)

You must obtain a **seller's permit** (re-sale number) if you:

Are engaged in business in California and Intend to sell or lease tangible personal property that would ordinarily be subject to sales tax if sold at retail.

The requirement to obtain a seller's permit applies to individuals as well as corporations, partnerships, and limited liability companies. Both wholesalers and retailers must apply for a permit.

If you do not hold a seller's permit and will make sales during temporary periods, such as Christmas tree sales and rummage sales, you must apply for a temporary seller's permit. Such permits are normally issued to selling operations lasting no longer than 30 days at one location.

WHAT DOES ENGAGED IN BUSINESS MEAN?

In California you are engaged in business if you:

Have an office, sales room, warehouse, or other place of business in this state (even if the location is only temporary).

Have a sales representative, agent, or canvasser operating in this state.

Receive rental payments from the lease of tangible personal property in this state.

There are other activities that may qualify a selling operation as being engaged in business in California. Due to the various rules that apply, you should contact the BOE's Information Center **800-400-7115** or contact your nearest BOE office to determine if you must obtain a permit.

What Is Ordinarily Subject to Sales Tax?
In general, retail sales of tangible personal property in California are subject to sales tax. Examples of tangible personal property include such items as furniture, giftware, toys, antiques, clothing, and so forth.

In addition, some service and labor costs are taxable if they result in the creation of tangible personal property. For example, if you make a ring for a specific customer, you are creating tangible personal property. Therefore, the total amount you charge for the ring (including the charge for labor) would be taxable

Reporting and Paying Sales Tax Don't panic. A list of how much to charge will be on the site. Just look up the city where the event is taking place and write down what percentage you will need to charge on each sale. You can file on-line or print off the form for filing and the instructions are very user friendly.

Practically speaking, you probably don't need a permanent sales permit unless you are making many sales. If you only do one or two booth events a year, a temporary sales permit will probably serve your purpose. However, the temporary permit requires you to file and pay the sales tax collected immediately after the event. To obtain the re-sale number simply go to the State Board of Equalization's website and download the form and instructions. If you travel out of state to make sales, you are going to need a separate permit for each state and report the sales to the individual states.

What Is A Sales and Use Tax Return? A sales and use tax return is used by seller's permit holders to report the payment of sales and use taxes to the BOE. Permit holders are required to file a tax return. Electronic Filing (e-filing) is the BOE's prescribed method for filing sales and use tax returns.

When Do I File? When you obtain your seller's permit, you will be instructed to file your tax return on a monthly, quarterly, or annual reporting basis.

Your tax return is due after the close of each reporting period. In other words, if your period closes on June 30, your tax return and payment is due on July 31, the last day of the following month. If the due date falls on a Saturday, Sunday or legal holiday, returns are due the following business day. Check the Calendar of Due Dates for your filing basis.

You must file your tax return and pay by the tax due date whether you efile, mail, or hand-deliver the return. Failure to receive a return or reminder from us does not excuse you from the requirement to file.

INSURANCE REQUIREMENTS

Insurance questions cannot be answered by anyone other than your insurance carrier. At a minimum, you probably want some sort of theft and personal liability coverage, but you will need to ask your insurance agent what your state requires or recommends. The event venue may have requirements for coverage also; they may want a rider from your company naming them as an additional insured for the day of the event. Whatever their requirements are—***get it in writing!***

How to find affordable art insurance coverage? Your regular carrier might not have contacts in this area; However, Local art groups have to carry event insurance for their art shows. Get in touch with them and ask for a referral to their insurance carrier. The carrier they are using may be a lot less expensive than someone unfamiliar with this type of coverage.

Questions to Ask what protection do I as a vendor need for my art and my possessions? What protection do I need if someone is hurt within my stall? What protection does the venue carry for fire, theft, personal liability? What about fire or other damage caused by an accident in another person's booth that then adversely affects mine? Ask all the "what if" questions you can think of and then make your own determination about participating. Also, check into whether there is an insurance contract and what the terms of the contract may be before signing and have your insurance agent look it over first as well as an attorney if there are things you don't understand. Never assume, always ask for clarifications and ***get them in writing***.

DID YOU MAKE MONEY?

There are other considerations besides profit that should go into making this decision. The type of the event should weigh heavily; if this is a major art-oriented event, it may mean that you will need to build up your artistic presence before you attract buyers. The type of art buyers are seeking at the event. If you are producing avant-garde art and the majority of the artists are selling more traditional styles this may not be the event for you. After each event you attend, you should do your own reviewing. Using the chart on the following page, rate the event using the following 10 - 1 scale, with a 10 being excellent, 5 being good or okay, and a 1 as poor using the questions provided. Feel free to add any questions you feel are relevant to your own experience.

For most artists, this is the most difficult part of an event to judge. Most of us simply aren't "right-brained" people! However, I have a simple formula I use when I decide if I made a profit on an event.

Expenses

- Cost of entry fee
- ·Mileage traveled to and from the event (here I use the IRS standard)
- Meals
- Gas for vehicle
- Lodging if I stay overnight
- Special Expenses (this is any expense required for the event I normally wouldn't have on hand)

Total Expenses

Profit

- Gross Sales
- Sales Tax collected
- Commission (sometimes an event requires a commission on your sales or a donation of some type)

Net Profit (gross sales minus taxes & commission)

DID YOU MAKE A PROFIT?

How to figure your Net Profit (gross sales minus taxes & commission) Sample below.

- **Expenses**
- Cost of entry fee $300.00
- Mileage traveled to and from the event (here I use the IRS standard) $19.60
- Meals $100.00
- Gas for vehicle $100.00
- Lodging if I stay overnight $300.00
- Special Expenses (this is any expense required for the event I normally wouldn't have on hand) $25.00
- Total Expenses $844.60

- **Profit**
- Gross Sales $1,500.00
- Sales Tax collected $123.38
- Commission (sometimes an event requires a commission on your sales or a donation of some type) ($150.00)
- Gross Profit $1,473.38
- Net Profit $628.78

SELLING ORIGINAL ART AT A NUTS & BOLTS EVENT

Copyright issues are always a risk for artists. If you sell a piece of your original art, the buyer needs to know that you are retaining the copyright. This is very important if you are attending an event catering primarily to the sale of art. While copyright laws do state that you are automatically covered, many consumers aren't aware that they need to pay you if they use your work on a commercial basis. I have included a sample of a receipt for an original art sale. Adapt it for your use and have several copies made up to take with you, when you make a sale, keep one copy for yourself and one for the buyer. downloadable PDFs of the resources can also be ordered on a single basis at these websites: www.gaildaleysfineart.com,

www.thepracticalartist.com and www.art-tique.org.

SAMPLE SALES RECEIPT

SALES RECEIPT

Date: ____________

Receipt No: ____________

Artist Name: ____________

Gallery Name ____________

Address: ____________

____

SOLD TO

____

Address

____

____

Phone No ____________

The Artist retains copyright of all Art listed on this receipt. No prints, copies, Internet distribution or video presentation of artwork may be done without the express written permission of the artist. The Purchaser will not permit any intentional destruction, damage or modification of the Art .A notice, must be permanently affixed to the Art, warning that copyright, ownership, etc., are subject to this contract. If the art is sold, the new owner shall be bound to these terms as if he had signed a sales agreement when he acquired the Art. This contract binds the parties, their heirs, and all their successors in interest, and all the Purchaser's obligations are attached to the Art and go with ownership of the art, all for the life of the Artist and the Artists surviving spouse plus 21 years. In any proceeding to enforce any part of this contract, the aggrieved party shall be entitled to reasonable attorney's fees in addition to any available remedy.

PAYMENT METHOD	CHECK NO.

QUANTITY	ITEM #	TITLE	UNIT PRICE	DISCOUNT	LINE TOTAL
			Total Discount		
				Subtotal	
				Sales Tax	
				Total	

THANK YOU FOR YOUR BUSINESS!

YOUR LOGO HERE

[Your company sloan]

MAKING RESIDUAL INCOME

Selling your books or art at craft shows and book signings isn’t the only way to make money off your work.

If you are a writer, you can make sales of the same item both as an e-book and in the printed form over and over. All you need is a sales platform. (More about this later).

Artists on the other hand, only create and sell a painting once, but they can still make multiple sales by selling prints of it.

In today's climate of social distancing, selling original art in person is very difficult. It's important to remember that art can still be sold. You can sell prints of your work or create a virtual gallery on-line. This section concentrates on being able to create residual income from your art. In Art Show Basics I discuss creating a residual gallery for your work.

We may as well admit it: all of us secretly want to not only create fabulous art but want the public to appreciate it so much they pay us fabulous prices for it. The wonderful thing about making prints of our work is it a way to earn residual income on our art. If an artist sells a painting for $500 that is a one-time fee; if that same artist also sells 20 prints for $15 each then they have earned a total of $800 on that same painting. Naturally as an artist, you want any reproductions of your art to reflect the quality of the art itself, which means you want to make the best quality reproductions you can find. I have had several artists ask me where they can get good quality prints made at a reasonable price. It's a good question. There are two ways to go with this: make the prints yourself or get them made professionally.

If you are planning to make them yourself, besides the printer, you will need a good quality camera that takes high-resolution photos (Canon Rebel is excellent but there are others out there). I don't recommend a point-and-shoot camera or your cell phone if you intend to make professional looking reproductions; although the smart phone photo quality is improving, I did notice that quality seemed to suffer with larger size prints. I would also recommend a good photo-editing program such as Photoshop Elements. I chose Elements because it will service either Apple or PC computers, the basic editing techniques are simple, and it does have tutorials.

A printer that prints on a variety of paper products is essential if you are making your own prints. What brand of printer makes the best prints? Well, there are a lot of differing opinions on this, all having to do with what kind of ink will give you the truest colors, how easy they are to use, whether to use ink jet or laser printers, etc. Making the prints yourself does mean that you are probably going to be limited to paper and the sizes you can make; most home printers will only take legal or letter size paper. The printer that gave me the very best prints I ever made at home was an inexpensive Kodak printer. Unfortunately, it proved too fragile to last long. Epson, Brother and HP all make good machines that will give you nice paper prints. You can even obtain letter size “canvas paper’ for printing on the internet, although I wasn’t really happy with the quality of the prints, I made with it on my home printer. If you are going to make prints yourself, you should consider the cost of the ink. Many ink jet printers devour ink pods like a T-Rex. If you make a lot of reproductions, Ink jet refills can be so expensive that you might find it less costly to get your prints made by a print shop. Laser printers also make good quality prints, but a color laser printer and the toner to go with it can also break your budget. You will need to decide if the cost of the printing will allow you to still make sales at a profit.

The next option is to have your prints made by a professional printer. I am speaking here of commercial printers such as Kinkos or CopyMax/Impress. The photo departments of Costco, Walgreens, Wal-Mart etc. may not give you a professional quality print because their print programs are designed to “flatten or homogenize” color to an “average” standard, however they also will work with you on this issue because they want your return business. Most of them can also do a canvas print mounted on stretcher bars. Again, ask for a proof because if you have vibrant, saturated or delicate shades you may find your print simply doesn’t reflect these qualities.

To use an outside printer, you need a high-resolution jpeg or other type of photo of your work. If you are not a photographer, I suggest you arrange to have a professional take the photo in order to ensure that the photo has no distortions and that the color is true to the original art. You can have the photo transferred to either a jump drive or disc. An issue with having your prints made by someone else that doesn’t come up with DIY (Do It Yourself) printing: calibrating their printer to your photos. Calibrating a printer has nothing to do with the printer type; it has to do with communication between the computer and the printer. Even if the photo from your thumb disc looks okay on their computer screen, the print may still come out darker or lighter than your art. Always ask for a proof before accepting the print because it may be necessary for you to take your disc or jump drive home so that you can adjust the lighting or color of the photo in order to make the print "true" to the original when using an outside printer. If you do this, always save the "adjusted" photo as a separate file and leave the original alone. Making these changes is much easier if you are dealing with a local printer.

The other option for having your prints made is to find a local professional who specializes in making art prints. Here in Fresno, we have several, but Mullins Photography is the one most favored by local artists. If you bring in your art, they make their own scan and reproduce a print that is virtually identical to the original. Ask other local artists in your area where they get their prints made. Be prepared to open your wallet for this option though; because the cost of the initial set up fee will be more expensive than say Kinkos or Impress. On the other hand, it probably will be a one-time fee for that particular piece of art and the quality will be the best.

You can also order prints from the internet; a number of Internet sites do on-line printing. These sites are sometimes referred to as POD (Print On Demand) sites, and most of them do an excellent job. Fine Art America for instance will not only make your prints on a variety of paper, metal, cards and canvas, but also sell matting and framing and ship to your customer. With on-line printers however, you will have the same difficulties with the calibration as with your local outside printer. Since you can't demand a proof from this type of site, I would suggest you get a small print made for yourself and adjust the photo.

Keep notes on what you did so that you can use them when sending in later prints. The nice thing about most POD sites is your customer may order directly from the site without you having to deal with nasty stuff like figuring out shipping costs.

SELLING BOOKS & ART DURING LOCKDOWN

Brick and Mortar art shows, galleries and bookstores had to make changes to adapt to the current crisis. Going to a crowded art show reception or visiting a Gallery during one are not healthy options under Covid 19. The same is true for holding a book signing or visiting a bookstore in person. However, writers, artists and galleries can still sell art and books. The key here is creating a virtual tour of your art, books or gallery.

How do you do this? Well, the first thing you need is photos of the art or your book covers. Make sure each photo is clear and the colors are true to the original. Use Photoshop (or any software photo editing program) to make sure the art isn't distorted.

Now create a script to accompany the presentation. I recommend using a script because it will help you to streamline the wording, stay on topic and remember essential items like how the viewer can actually purchase what you are trying to sell.

Now you are ready to generate your presentation. I suggest you use a good presentation program to do this. While not all presentation programs are created equal, most of them do come with tutorials, and some with a free trial.

You might not get it right the first time but stay with it. You want to be able to post your finished presentation on your website and on social media sites like

Facebook, LinkedIn, Instagram, Twitter and Instagram to name only a few, so check the format used by each site. It might not be the same for all of them.

Below is a list of a few of them: Click on the link below to check them out.

FREE SOFTWARE SITES TO CREATE A PRESENTATION

https://listoffreeware.com/list-of-best-free-software-to-create-presentations/

- **MagicLantern** is a free presentation application and can be used as an alternative to Microsoft PowerPoint.
- Sparkol is a free software for creating multimedia presentations. This freeware gives a classy touch to your presentations.
- _is free presentation software used to build cool slideshows by inserting animation, 2D & 3D clip art, using advance drawing tools and master slides.
- PDF Presenter is a free software to create presentations by using PDF documents.

- www.canva.com/Presentation/Creator **This One Has a Free trial version** Create A Standout **Presentation** In Minutes With Canva's **Presentation** Creator. Try It Now!

TIPS ON PHOTOGRAPHING YOUR ART

Presentation is everything; especially on the internet where the only impression you can make is what is seen by the viewer. A poor presentation can make the difference between getting a sale or not and being accepted into an on-line show or a show requiring submissions on disc. For the judge or a buyer to get an accurate idea of your art, the image you send must match the colors in the art and be sharp and clear.

For many of us, taking a good photograph of our art is hard. Before sending off the photo of your art your art, make sure that the size of the photo agrees with the directions given by the prospectus, and that the image is sharp, clear and not distorted. Then check the colors in the photo against the actual art to make sure they are correct. I am not a professional photographer, but I do manage to take credible photos of my work without paying a pro to do it for me. Even if you are only making a record of your work, you will want it to be as close to the original as possible. Here are a few tips that might help those of us who are "photo challenged".

LIGHTING

Take the photo in an area that doesn't cast shadows or cause glares on the work. Personally, I prefer to take my photos outside on a clear day using indirect sunlight, but since most art will be displayed indoors, indoor lighting is also okay. I don't use an elaborate set up; I have simply put nails into the Garage Door at the appropriate height for the camera and then I rest the painting's stretcher bars on the nails. If you are using paper or canvas sheets, you can attach the sticky stuff teachers use to hang students' artwork on the wall to the back of the art (after making sure your art is level).

Check that the sun isn't glaring on the work so there are no shinny surfaces to reflect back at the camera lens. If you are working with watercolor or pastel, then take the photo before you frame it because glass will reflect back at the camera. I also take the photo before I varnish acrylics to cut down on the glare caused by the varnish. Oils are naturally shiny so be extra careful no bright light shows in the photo.

If your camera is set up to put a polarizing filter over the lens, it may be worth your while to buy one, especially if you work in Oil paints or other naturally shiny mediums. If your camera won't take a filter, you can try the "poor man's sub" and buy a pair of polarizing sunglasses and put them in front of your lens. The only real issue I see with this cheap fix is that the lens on the sunglasses may not be flat and so create a bubble effect on the photo.

DISTORTION

In order to avoid distorting the image, the art should be hung on a flat surface. If the final photo is wider at the bottom than the top or vice versa, perhaps your hanging surface isn't flat, and you will need to take corrective action in your photo-editing program or find another surface.

Aim your camera squarely at the art. It helps to use a tripod; you can align the front two feet of the tripod squarely with the art so that you aren't taking the photo at an angle that will cause one side of the art to be larger than the other. If necessary, use a tape measure to make sure the feet are an equal distance from the art, and check that the camera isn't twisted on the tripod. A tripod also helps to prevent blurring is caused by your hand shaking. Most of us don't think our hand moves when pushing the button, but it does.

Use a small hand level to ensure that the camera is not angled either down or up when taking the photo as this will also cause distortion. A laser pointer (your pets' toy is adequate) laid alongside the lens when measuring will also help you to line up your lens on your art.

CAMERAS

You don't need an expensive camera just to take photos of your art. Canon makes an excellent quality digital camera for under $300 and it is very user friendly. As a plus, the newer models also take video so you can use the video setting to record art shows or yourself when creating the art, and then upload to Facebook, U-tube and other social network sites.

However, if you are planning to make large-size reproductions of your work then a good SLR camera should be on your list. SLR stands for single-lens reflex. This type of camera allows you take enormous photos, which translate well into prints as large as 48 x 60 without blurring.

The newer smart phones also take adequate photos if all you want is a good photo of your art and don't intend to use the photo to make prints to sell. Unfortunately, cell phone makers don't have a cell phone on the market that will take a photo with enough pixels to be useful for full size prints. Someday, maybe, but not quite yet.

CAMERA SETTINGS

When taking the initial (raw) photo of your work, be sure to set your camera to take fine or large files and take at least 3 exposures of each artwork.

EDITING PHOTOS

I find the least expensive and easiest to use photo-editing program, is Adobe Photoshop. It has tutorials and is easy to learn. Before making any additional copies, check for any corrective actions that you need to take; you can then make additional copies at different resolutions.

Look first for distortions. Photoshop makes it easy to correct the distortions caused by not having your camera lined up correctly with the artwork.

Next, check the contrast of the photo against the original if is dull then increase the contrast if necessary.

The next step is to check the actual color and correct it if the image shows too much blue, green or red.

Your last step should be to crop the photo of your work so that only the work shows. I usually also crop a very tiny piece of the edges as well to keep the curve on the edge of my canvas from appearing as a distortion. Then save the photo as a PDF so you can go back to it in its original form. Save it again as a tiff image and then as a jpeg. You will be working with the jpeg format, but this format does develop a slight blurring or distortion when saved multiple times.

YOU NEED THREE IMAGE SIZES

Image No 1 should be a large resolution image (between 1 and 2 MB between 300 - 600 pixels per inch) POD sites usually demand a large high-resolution image to make prints; usually between 38,000 and 60,000 pixels on a side.

Image No 2 should be a medium/low resolution image to put on your website and submit to prospective galleries or anyone else who needs to see your work. This size is (between 1 - 2 KB at 72 pixels/inch or adjust the widest side to be between 7 and 10 inches) and will be large enough to allow the viewer to see the art. It is too small to encourage attempts to pirate your image because it probably won’t make prints any larger than a 5 x 7 without blurring, but you can add digital watermarking with Elements or other watermarking programs.

Image No 3 should be small image (between 200 and 125 pixels at the widest edge) for thumbnail images and record keeping; for those of you who prefer sizes given in inches, the widest edge should be no more than 4”.

Keep a photo log with both high- and low-resolution photos of your work separately from your desktop computer; the new flash drives are excellent for this or you can use one of the on-line backup programs. A working copy can be kept on your desktop or tablet but be sure and back up your files each month onto a separate disc or jump drive. Keep the back-up copies of these items in a separate place and up-date your back-ups monthly. There are also some cloud features that will enable you to automatically back-up your digital files (for a price). While these are handy to use, if you are late paying the monthly fee, how do you reclaim your images? Once your records are lost due to computer crashes, natural disaster or any other reason they are gone. I consider it vitally important to have an off-line storage of my art photos.

TIPS ON PRICING ART

Let’s talk pricing. In my work as Art-tique.org Director, I am often asked by artists who are just starting out how much they should charge for their work. I always tell beginning artists that art pricing is personal (meaning every artist pretty much makes up their own rules!). However, the one thing I think is most important:

Make sure the price of the art first covers the cost of your time and materials.

I tried the free art price calculator on the web, and found it interesting, although pricing art is so idiosyncratic that it wasn't really as useful as I had hoped.

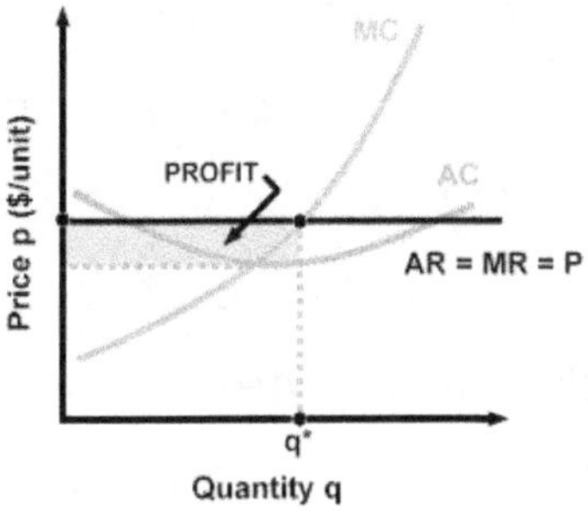

If you want to use the “per square inch” approach, you can emulate the Printing companies who do price by the square inch.

Take a survey (get prices) locally from both a high-end printer of Giclee and your local print shop (Kinkos, Office Impress) and check out the pricing on the on-line printer Fine Art America. Compare the prices.

If you don't want to use that approach, go to a local art show, compare your art to the winning art, and check out other artists' prices. This will give you a ballpark figure on how much other artists in your area are charging. Where prospective buyers will see the art does make a difference. I live in a large city surrounded by farming and agriculture that is not considered an art mecca for California. If I sell a painting in my area, I will get less for it than if I had marketed on the Coast because for some reason, buyers think that there is more 'cachet' from art bought in Carmel or San Francisco than that bought in Fresno. The same painting by the same artist will earn more if marketed in a pricey gallery in New York than it will in New Jersey.

When checking pricing at an art show, you should be looking for the following criteria: Artists who paint the same or similar subject matter (abstracts, still lifes, portraits, landscapes, etc.) Be honest: is your art as good as theirs is? If you don't know, ask a more experienced artist to critique your work. Please be careful with this; the person who does the critiquing should be a more experienced artist with some know

ledge of technique and the principles of art. We love them, but the opinions of our friends and family who don't know any more than we do about art really aren't useful as critiques.

Enter some art shows and have a professional (a paid judge) give you an honest opinion.

Lastly, how much do you like the art? If you really like it, don't give it away. Price it so that you will be happy if it sells, not regret that you gave it away.

If it doesn't sell, you can enjoy looking at it!

If you are still interested in using the art price calculator, here a couple of links to free art pricing sites.

http://www.artscope.net/artworth.html

Or

http://www.artpricecalculator.com/

MARKETING TIPS FOR AUTHORS

PRICING

To price your books to sell, you need to do your research. In order to attract readers, your books need pricing that is in line with other books in your genre. If an author already has an established following, they can get away with higher prices. A Nora Roberts e-book for instance might be priced as high as $14.99. But Nora has a big reader fan club and most of her fans will pay that. For those of you who *don't* have that kind of following, I suggest pricing an e-book anywhere from $2.99 to $4.99. Softcover Trade paperbacks (6" x 9") usually go for around $13 to $15 dollars.

KNOW YOUR BOOK

Look at the book as if you are a completely new reader and answer these questions: What is it about? What Genre is it? Is it similar to other books in the same Genre? Who what are potential readers and what are they interested in?

What metadata are you using? Metadata simply means “data about data”. It is information about your book not in the story (Cover, title, traditional blurb and tags to make it easier to be found by a search engine).

ELEVATOR PITCH OR TAGLINE

A Tagline is a one- or two-line phrase designed to hook a potential reader into looking at your book. I struggle with this myself so the best way I’ve found is to try and put the blurb into a haiku (a Japanese poem of seventeen syllables, in three lines of five, seven, and five words).

ADVERTISING & PUBLICITY

You can pay out a lot of money for advertising, and this is fine. Amazon in particular has some great paid advertising. However effective advertising doesn’t have to be paid. Social Media is a great way to advertise your books, and you can make an ad yourself on BookBrush.com at no cost. Joining in a multi-author promotion is another way this can be done. Two of my favorite sites for this are BookBub.com and AuthorsXPromotions.com both of whom have promotions to also help you build up an e-mail list. You also need a web site to advertise your books. It doesn't need to be an expensive one; several host sites have a free option (FYI: these usually come with 3rd party ads). An author page on Facebook will help to promote your books as well.

BOOK COVERS

We've all heard the phrase "don't judge a book by its cover". Everyone who looks at a book does this. Your book cover is one of the most important "hooks" you have to get noticed by readers. The cover is actually the first page of your story; it tells potential readers about the style and mood of the book. Would Stephen King's "Cemetery" have sold if he had used an illustrated cover commonly found in Cozy Mysteries? Romance and Erotica genres make good use of these tropes by using attractive models clutching each other on the covers. A good cover design draws a reader's attention and involves them emotionally.

Your book cover should look professional. A few of the things marking a book cover as "unprofessional" are: 1) A font that is hard to read from a distance and in a thumbnail (the small version of your cover that shows on Amazon). Bad covers might have pixelated images, visible watermarks, badly formatted or aligned text. These are a no–no. Aside from getting you kicked off of a multi-level promotion, they hint bad things about the interior of your book.

KISS Simple is better. A cluttered cover can detract from the appearance of your book. It will make your title harder to find.

POOR FORMATTING

A poorly formatted interior can also spell disaster. Here are a few things that constitute poor formatting. 1) Using unjustified or rag-right typesetting. 2) Mixed formatting (using block style or not indenting the first line and instead separating each paragraph with a line) while block formatting is usually acceptable in non-fiction or a textbook, it isn't found in well formatted fiction. Fiction novels customarily indent the first line of each paragraph and do not skip a line between them. 3) Watch your page numbering. Odd numbered pages should always be on the right (unless you are writing Aniame in which case the rules are entirely different). 4) Making super small margins to save money on printing. Always use "mirror" margins (the inside and outside of alternating pages are different). When converting your manuscript to an ePub or Mobi, often the formatting will change and sometimes the font as well. I suggest using one of the common fonts for an e-book. If you want the larger, easier to read font for paperback or hardback books, change the font to one of these and submit your manuscript in PDF when uploading to a distribution site.

CREATING AN ATTRACTIVE COVER

Your cover should have a strong composition, an intriguing focal point, clear title and subtitles on a simplistic background.

A GOOD TITLE

A few points: 1) Make the title large enough to be read clearly. 2) It should look at home on the cover. Your title font should coinside with your's books message, it's tone and your reading audience. 3) It should stand out from the cover art (use a contrasting color on the Title font). 4) Less is more. 5) You aren't required to use the same font for the title, tag line or author's name, but avoid using more than two different ones. 5) Use a font that look similar (but not an exact copy) as those used in books in the same genre. A good way to research this is to put in your genre and add "best sellers" into Amazon's search engine.

TEASERS ON THE COVER

This can be a subtitle, a quote, a tag line or something that hints at the plot.

If possible, incorporate keywords into the title.

BACKGROUND IMAGE

Color is the first thing. While dark or muted colors are the norm with certain genres (steampunk often uses sepia and post-apocalyptic generally uses dark backgrounds) touches of bright colors will attract a potential reader's attention and make your book stand out. Romance genres generally have a light background or softer colors. Do your research on Amazon or other bookstore sites. You can also check out Goodreads, Pinterest or Google book cover ideas.

STEPS TO CREATE YOUR OWN COVER

REASEARCH

If you find the task of creating a cover daunting, you can always hire a professional to create one for you. If you go this route, be sure and check out your designer's experience in making covers in your chosen genre. A designer used to creating Cozy Mystery covers might not be a good choice for a book in the western or horror genre.

FINDING USABLE IMAGES

Using a site that has free or low-priced stock photos is the best place to find a potential background cover. Some free sites are: Stocksnap.io, Burst, Pexels (FYI—this is NOT the same site as Pixels which is a Fine Art America site), Upsplash, PrimoPrint, Pixabay, FoodiesFeed, Freestocks.org, and Picography.

Shutterstock.com is one of the best places to find low-priced stock images, these are also good: Adobe Stock photos, Getty Images, iStock, StoryBlocks, Kate Max Stock, Stock Unlimited and Haute Stock.

BOOK COVER SIZES

Your cover image must fit on your book without looking distorted. The most common softcover book size is 6" x 9" (Trade Paperback) the spine on the cover will vary depending on how many pages in your book. If you pick out a background cover that is in landscape (horizontal) mode, it will have to be cropped to prevent distortion.

There are several excellent cover design options both free and paid out there. Amazon offers a free cover design template, but I found it difficult to use. Create space had a great one, but unfortunately when it was eaten by Amazon a few years ago, Amazon discarded their user-friendly version and substituted the one they now use. BookBrush and Canva both offer cover design features at a low monthly/yearly price.

Here a few free book cover designs software to use:

- Canva
- Adobe Spark
- Graphic Springs
- DIY Book Covers
- Design Wizard
- GIMP
- Venngage Book Cover Maker

The following are paid advanced software designs

- Photoshop - $9.99/months
- Adobe Illustrator - $31.49/month
- Pic Monkey - $7.99/month to $12.99/month

TEST YOUR COVER

It's a good idea to create several versions of your cover and test them on an audience. You can pay a site to do this, or Facebook has several Groups you can join who will critique your covers for free.

- Indie Cover Project
- Indie Book Cover CLEAN Sales & Design
- Book Cover Designer Events
- Indie Writers Unite
- Author Tree
- Book Cover Gallery

This is not all of the Facebook groups who will critique your design. There are also groups specializing in pre-made covers (FYI: these are for sale).

MOST USEFUL SITES FOR WRITERS:

The world of self-publishing can be scary. As an independent author publishing your own stuff, there are 3 types of sites you need to take your book from your desk to bookstores: Creation sites, Editing Sites, and Promotional sites. There are loads of sites out there for aspiring writers to use. Some of them are very expensive and some are more middle of the road. I haven't found a lot of free sites that were actually useful, but there are some good ones if you know what to look for. I am a starving writer, so I tend to go for what will give me the most bang for the money I spend.

This is a list of the sites I have found the most useful:

BOOK RESEARCH

Best Overall Generator for just about anything: Fantasy Name Generator. It’s a Free Site although they do want you to share it on social media. This one isn't only for fantasy writers. It actually has plenty of other generators such as "backstory descriptions, battlefield descriptions, city descriptions; even a calendar creator!

https://www.fantasynamegenerators.com/#other

GRAMMAR & SPELLING

PROWRITINGAID.COM.

ITS Not free, although they have a free option you can try out. FYI its spell check is based on British English so some spelling it checks will simply be the difference between American spelling and that used in the British Isles. The site will find style errors, checks for readability, etc. and give you the option of ignoring the issue or fixing it.

MAKE YOUR OWN COVER

You can get a proto design a cover for you (See Fiverr.com for an inexpensive site) or if you are skilled with graphics, you can make your own. Before you do this, I strongly urge you do some research on

Amazon and take a good hard look at the covers of books selling in your genre. FYI the simpler the design the better. Don't make the mistake of attempting to put too much information on the cover. A single quote is okay in addition to the title and your name as an author, but any more will detract from the artwork you are using to pull in your readers.

Creating an e-book cover isn't hard; just make sure your design is about 300 pixels per inch so it will enlarge without looking fuzzy. You can resize it in your photo editing program to fit the size. The usual size for a book cover is either 6w x 9H or 5.5w x 8.5H. A paperback cover is a lot more difficult. The spine width is different for each book because the width is determined by the number of pages in the book. If you use Draft2Digital, they will create a paperback cover using the one you uploaded for the e-book. If you use Amazon, you will have to go to their Author site, put in the number of pages in your book and download a template to cut and paste in your front, back and spine covers.

SHUTTERSTOCK

This is a marketing site for artists, photographers, or graphic creators to market their work. The user pays $50 for five downloads (covers the royalty for the creator of the picture you download). It has literally hundreds of photos, vectors or art available. I use it primarily as a source for covers for my books.

NEXMUSE.

This is a site that enables you to alter or change the photograph you have chosen for the cover. It alters the photo. The site has a free option although you can upgrade to the paid format which gives you more options.

DISTRIBUTION & BOOK FORMATTING

There are two types of distribution used by publishers. Amazon and what are termed 'wide' Sites. When you use wide publication, it means you market your books in as many formats to as many different companies as you can. Here in America, we have the big three, I-Books, Amazon and Nook, although Kobo is coming up fast on the outside. The two kinds of formatting used are e-pub and Mobi, which is where using a 'wide' distributor like Draft2Digital shines.

CONVERTIO

This is a site for converting your document to either e-Pub, Mobi, or a variety of other formats. I've found this one especially useful for creating excerpts of my books that I can send to potential readers or reviewers. Very User Friendly.

DRAFT2DIGITAL

Its free to use. D2D will take a percentage of your royalty sales. This is a 'wide' distributor of e-books, they convert your book to PDF, e-Pub or Mobi and submit it over 20 sites (Nook, Kobo, Amazon, I-Books, etc.).

PROMOTIONAL SITES

Let's face it, if you are an independent publisher there is a lot more to getting your books out there than just writing them. You also have to wear the advertising hat. You have to create your own ads (or pay another independent to do this for you) and you need a schedule to remind you when you've agreed to share the promotion.

BOOK BRUSH

For a yearly fee, this site has templates to help you create book covers, social media ads (Facebook, Twitter, Instagram, etc.), bookmarks, etc.

FIVERR.COM

Is a site with hundreds of graphic artists, digital marketing, writing and translation, video and animation, etc. that you can search through to find the expert you need. Prices range from $25 to over $300. The creators set their own pricing and you can select how much you are willing to pay for the service they offer.

BOOK FUNNEL.

It's a promotional site; authors join promotions with a group of other authors. This part is free, but it's a quid pro quo type of site. You share the entire promotion with your e-mail list and on social media. This is a mid-range site as far as pricing goes. The cheapest option is $29 which is great for first time writers to get their feet wet on. I chose the mid-range site $100, which allows me to collect the e-mail addresses of folks who liked my books.

AUTHORSXPROMOTION

As you might have guessed, this is a promotional site. Its free to join but you pay an average of $55 for each promotion you take a part in. The promotions are setup as a lottery; readers are randomly picked to receive 1 free book from all the authors (Grand Prize) and 1 e-book or paperback is given to a winner who selected your book if they win. Maximum giveaway 3 free books. It’s a good site for expanding your e-mail list; I picked up around 600 new e-mails on the one I joined.

USING AN AGENT

Unfortunately, I don't have a site with lists of agents to submit to. Beware of scams in this area. If the guy (or gal) you're talking to tells you to order books for distribution (for which you pay) Watch Out! Some sites infamous for using this tactic can be found using this link:

https://www.victoriastrauss.com/2018/01/19/solicitation-alert-book-art-press-solutions-and-window-press-club-2/

ABOUT THE AUTHOR

Gail Daley is a self-taught artist and writer with a background in business. An omnivorous reader, she was inspired by her son, also a writer, to finish some of the incomplete novels she had begun over the years. She is heavily involved in local art groups and fills her time reading, writing, painting in acrylics, and spending time with her husband of 45 plus years. Currently her family is owned by two cats, a mischievous kitten called Mab (after the fairy queen of air and darkness) and a mellow Gray Princess named Moonstone. In the past, the family shared their home with many dogs, cats and a Guinea Pig, all of whom have passed over the rainbow bridge. A recent surgery and a bout with breast cancer have slowed her down a little, but she continues to write and paint.

OTHER BOOKS BY GAIL DALEY

SPACE COLONY JOURNALS

Options Of Survival
Destiny Rising
Tomorrows Legacy
The Interstellar Jewel Heist
The Designer People
Alien Trails
Quantum Light

PORTAL WORLD TALES

ST. ANTONI - THE FORBIDDEN COLONY

Warriors of St. Antoni
The Enforcers
The Gaslight Bandits
The Portal Lawman
Cradle of Fire
The Clone Initiative*

MAGI OF RULARI

Spell Of The Magi
Magi Storm
Magi Paladin*

NON-FICTION

The Complete Modern Artist's Handbook

PAMPHLETS

Introduction To The Internet #1
The Hard Stuff - Handbook #2
Art Show Basics - Handbook #3
Framing on a Budget - Handbook #4
Are You Making Money? - Handbook #5

Are You Making Money - The Modern Artists Handbook - Vol 5

*In the works. Publication date to be announced.

NOTES

www.ingramcontent.com/pod-product-compliance
Lightning Source LLC
Chambersburg PA
CBHW071241170526
45165CB00003B/1192